Sissy
Goes
Tiny

Sissy Goes Tiny

Editor: Mallory Adamson

Graphics and Cover Design: meadencreative.com

First Edition 2019

Library of Congress Cataloging-in Publication Data on record.

ISBN 978-1-936426-22-5

19 20 21 22 LSC/C 10 9 8 7 6 5 4 3 2 1

Audrey Press
P.O. Box 6113
Maryville, TN 37802

Dedications

For Jake and Sara; the two medium-sized humans who make me whole.

Rebecca Flansburg

Every day I am thankful for my parents, Ray & Gladys, who somehow instilled in me the belief that I am capable of doing whatever I set my mind to.

BA Norrdgard

Sissy
Goes
Tiny

WRITTEN BY

REBECCA FLANSBURG
and BA NORRGARD

ILLUSTRATED BY

PENNY WEBER

⊛ AUDREYPRESS

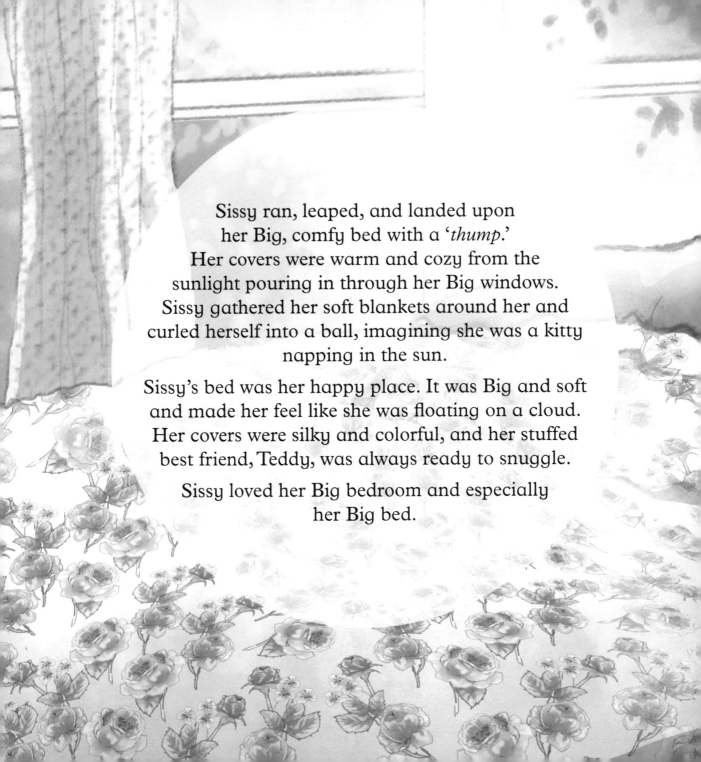

Sissy ran, leaped, and landed upon
her Big, comfy bed with a '*thump.*'
Her covers were warm and cozy from the
sunlight pouring in through her Big windows.
Sissy gathered her soft blankets around her and
curled herself into a ball, imagining she was a kitty
napping in the sun.

Sissy's bed was her happy place. It was Big and soft
and made her feel like she was floating on a cloud.
Her covers were silky and colorful, and her stuffed
best friend, Teddy, was always ready to snuggle.

Sissy loved her Big bedroom and especially
her Big bed.

Sissy also loved her life.

She loved her mommy and daddy.

She loved her Big house that was surrounded by Big oaks and Small chirping birds.

"My life is soooo perfect," she would think to herself as she stared at the clouds through her bedroom window. She was sure she heard Teddy agree as she pressed his furry face into hers.

Life felt *good*.

Then one day, her mommy and daddy appeared in the doorway of her room. In their hands, they held a Big book with a picture of a Little house on the cover.

A really Little house.

They all sat together on her Big comfy bed and Mommy wrapped her hands around Sissy's. "Your dad and I have been talking," she said, "and we've decided that we want our family to live Tiny."

"Live Tiny?" Sissy repeated in alarm. "We have to shrink ourselves?"

"No, honey," her daddy chuckled. "We aren't going to shrink ourselves, but we are going to shrink what we own.

We are 'going Tiny'—that means, as a family, we are selling our Big house and moving into a Smaller one—a much Smaller one.

Our new Tiny House will be on wheels, so we can travel and live wherever we want! Everywhere we go, we will always have our home with us. Living Tiny means we can own Fewer things and have More experiences."

Sissy was puzzled.

She eyed her dollhouse and secretly wondered
if her new home would be that Small.

Where would she put all her toys and clothes?
Would she even have her own room? "Going tiny"
didn't sound like very much fun. But…Mommy
and Daddy seemed very excited.

"Ok…" she muttered.
"But will I still have a
Huge backyard with Tall,
Tall trees? Will I still have
my Big comfy bed?"

"You won't just have *one* backyard, you'll have many! Our backyard will change as we discover new places, where we can explore and find new Big trees to climb," her mommy explained.

"And you will still have your own space for sleeping. It will be much Smaller, but it will be special—just like you! Now, to get ready for our new Tiny House adventure, we need to do some hard work as a family.

Living Tiny means we all need to learn to make do with Less. We must look at everything we own and keep only the things that have a necessary purpose or are very special to us. We're going to do what's called a possessions purge."

Purge? That was a scary word to Sissy's ears. But choosing to live with Fewer things, *that* she understood.

Her mind raced with visions of the things she would be happy to see go. Maybe Daddy would finally get rid of the ukulele that hurt her ears, and Mommy would stop hosting those fancy garden parties with weird food.

But when she thought of parting with some of her *own* possessions, she felt sad and scared all over again. This Tiny House thing didn't sound like much fun at all.

As the days whizzed by, Sissy became more and more optimistic about her family's new lifestyle. All the tasks and anticipation involved in going Tiny felt a lot like when they planned family vacations.

One afternoon, some friends who were already living Tiny stopped by and showed Sissy how she could repurpose some of her favorite things. The apron that Grandma had given her for Christmas could be remade into curtains for her room, and her favorite baby blanket would be made into a pillow for her new bed.

They showed Sissy how to use the shells that Auntie Janice brought her from Florida, along with the sparkly pretend jewelry that her friend Teagan gave her, to make a pretty sun catcher. Sissy wondered if it would sparkle and cast rainbows on the wall of her new Tiny room.

Their friends also taught them to take pictures of their Favorite Things, like their Big house, their Big yard, and even special places in their hometown to create a Memory Book. The book would save special memories forever, and, one day, Sissy and her parents could look back on their old life and compare it to their new, exciting one.

It was hard to say goodbye to many of her toys, but it made Sissy's heart happy when she and her family dropped them off at a special place where other Mommies and Daddies were trying to get a fresh start in their life. She knew her old toys would make a new child just as happy as they'd made her.

Her mommy and daddy were excited too, but they also struggled to get rid of some things.

She was sure her mommy had tears in her eyes when she said good-bye to her mixer (the one she only used at Christmas), and Daddy didn't look too happy when he gave his golf clubs to Mr. Ryan, the neighbor guy.

As the family purged their possessions, Sissy's daddy also explained that downsizing and "living with less" would give them a freedom they'd never had before. Mommy agreed and added that more is not better... living better is better.

"The more stuff you own, the more your stuff owns you," her daddy piped up as he proudly deposited three years' worth of magazines into the recycling bin.

Little by little, possession by possession, Sissy and her family's "Keep" pile kept getting Smaller, and their "Sell" and "Donate" piles kept getting Bigger.

And it felt *good*.

Then it happened.

The day came when Sissy's Big house was almost empty. It could have been her imagination, but Sissy was sure the air in her old home felt better and lighter. At the same time, though, it felt lonely and strange.

Just when Sissy was wondering if this whole Tiny House thing was really a good idea after all...

a Big truck pulled up with...

…their new Tiny House!

Sissy could barely contain her excitement as she not-so-patiently waited for their New Tiny House to be parked and secured.

Mommy and Daddy must have been excited too, because all three of them almost got stuck in the front door as they rushed together to get inside the place they would now call Home.

Sissy caught her breath in delight.

It was beautiful! More beautiful than her eight-year-old brain could have imagined. For a Tiny House it felt... Big! Things were tidy and compact, and everything had its place.

Sissy giggled when she saw that even the steps going up to the loft had drawers! She couldn't wait to explore all the parts of the Tiny house and discover all of its secret cubbies.

"Can you lose things in a Tiny House?" she wondered to herself.

Sissy raced up the stairs that led to her loft bedroom. The twinkle lights that used to be on her headboard were now wrapped around the handrail, and, just as she predicted, her homemade sun catcher glittered and danced in light that streamed in from her new skylight window.

As she looked around her new room, she saw only her most favorite things. The Tiny bookshelf above the bed held her very favorite books and some new ones too. The new books had titles like *Homeschooling Made Fun and State Park Junior Ranger*—hints at the adventures ahead.

Sissy flopped onto her new Tiny bed and happily wiggled her toes. Even though it was a brand new room, it felt like "her space." Downstairs she could hear Daddy saying that he was excited to have his own work space. Mommy chimed in that she was glad they didn't have to share any more.

Her new fold-out desk would be the perfect place to Skype friends and family from the road, she said. Sissy also heard them unrolling the colorful U.S.A. wall map, where they would put pins in for every place they visited.

Sissy sighed happily.
Life felt *good*.

She knew there would
be days when she missed
her old bed and many toys,
but she didn't feel sad about
it anymore. She also knew that
her family's new Tiny Living
adventure was full of Big
possibilities, and wherever they
stopped on their Journey, they
would always be Home.

Acknowledgments

We are incredibly grateful!

Grateful to have family, friends, and spouses who have cheered us on during the creation and publishing of *Sissy Goes Tiny*.

Grateful that Valarie Budayr, CEO of Audrey Press, saw the potential in this book and took us under her wing.

Grateful that we have creative and brilliant people like illustrator Penny Weber, book designer Andy Meaden, and editor Mallory Adamson in our corner — shepherding us towards the finish line (and beyond).

Grateful that this project was supported by Five Wings Arts Council with funds from the McKnight Foundation.

And grateful to be following in the footsteps of all of the luminaries and innovators in the tiny house community who show us daily what community really means while being advocates and examples of an unconventional style of living that is beneficial in so many ways (mental health and for Mother Earth!) We appreciate all of you in more ways than you will ever know!

History of Sissy and Fun Tiny House Facts

Tiny houses are typically around 300 square feet.

Tiny house communities are made up of mostly women in their 40s and 50s, but families are becoming more common.

Tiny house owners are choosing a simpler lifestyle. The primary motivation is financial and more personal freedom.

Sissy is named after co-author BA Norrgard's tiny house; Sisu. It's a Finnish word meaning having grit, determination, and perseverance in the face of adversity.

BA- *"I had my tiny home a few years before I named her and at, first, I couldn't think of a fitting name. Then my mom died. She was Finnish & she had a lot of sisu, and a name was suddenly clear."*

Rebecca Flansburg

Rebecca "Becky" Flansburg is an author, freelance writer and blogger from Minnesota who writes about parenthood topics and being a solopreneur. She is mom to two humans and critter mom to way too many pets. Rebecca credits her quick wit and positive outlook on life for keeping her sane and successful. She is a proud Board Member of Lakes Area Writers Alliance and readers can also find her at BeckyFlansburg.com or on Instagram.

BA Norrgard

In 2012, bucking societal exceptions and following her inner guidance, B.A. (Beth Ann) Norrgard shed her paralegal costume after 26 years in a downtown high rise and hand built her tiny house. She is a passionate advocate for others following their dreams and letting go of societal conditioning, and being free to live a larger life in a smaller space. BA is a doer. She has traveled over 14,000 miles with her house and writes about her minimalist, vegan life on her website, banorrgard.com

Penny Weber

Penny Weber is a full time illustrator from Long Island, New York, where she's lived all of her life. She creates digital illustrations that mimic the look of water color and traditional painting. Penny attended the School of Visual Arts in New York City where she studied graphic design and illustration. In 2007 quickly signed with Wendy Mays and Janice Onken to be represented by WendyLynn & Company, (www.wendylynn.com). Penny has illustrated many books for the trade and educational market.

AUTHOR BA Norrgard

AUTHOR Rebecca Flansburg

ILLUSTRATOR Penny Weber